KidLit-O

What's So Great About

Picasso?

A Guide to Pablo Picasso Just For Kids!

Max Tanner

KidLit-O Books

www.kidlito.com

© 2013. All Rights Reserved.

Cover Iamge © NLshop - Fotolia.com

Table of Contents

About KidCaps

KidLit-O is an imprint of BookCaps™ that is just for kids! Each month BookCaps will be releasing several books in this exciting imprint. Visit are website or like us on Facebook to see more!

To add your name to our mailing list, visit this link: **http://www.kidlito.com/mailing-list.html**

Introdcution

Many famous artists lived hundreds of years ago. It seems that, in the past hundred and fifty years, only a small handful of artists have ever become remotely popular. Modern art just seems not to be as captivating as older art is. There are plenty of familiar names from hundreds of years ago—Leonardo da Vinci, Vincent van Gogh, Michelangelo, and Raphael, among many others.

One of the leaders of the modern art movement was named Pablo Picasso, a Spanish artist, many of whose paintings are still majorly famous and widely reprinted today. Picasso is known for his unique painting styles, and also his involvement in history. Picasso lived within the past century and a half, during which many drastic history movements were taking place, such as the Spanish Civil War, World War I, World War II, and many other cultural events that shaped the world as we know it. Part of the reason that Picasso is so famous is because the link between his art and history at the time.

In order to understand his art, we must first understand his life and what his childhood was like. How did he start painting? How did he decide what to put down on canvases and paper? What about his art made people like it? How did he become famous? What role did his art play during the times of World War I, World War II, and the Spanish Civil War? Why did he spend most of his life in France? What is his enduring legacy?

Pablo Picasso was an intriguing man that led a fascinating life, and studying him is studying a hugely important part of history and culture. Picasso's story is a human story, and many readers will find that he is one of the most intriguing artists in the world.

Chapter 1: Childhood of the Artist

In the south of Spain, there is a city called Malaga. Today, it is one of the most populated cities in all of Spain. At the time, among thousands of other people, there were two remarkable people living in Malaga: one of them was José Ruiz y Blasco and the other was María Picasso y López. José was a painter and a teacher, and he often taught young students how to draw. María and José married each other in 1880, and one year later they had their first child.

The child's name was exceptionally long: Pablo Diego Jose Francisco de Paula Juan Nepomuceno Maria de los Remedios Cipriano de la Santisima Trinidad Ruiz y Picasso—or, for short, Pablo Picasso. Why were there so many names in Picasso's full name? During that time period, it was normal for parents to give their child several middle names, usually taken from family members or Catholic saints. Even today, the royal child born to Prince William and Duchess Kate Middleton was named George Alexander Louis. Although not as flashy as Picasso's name, in many families and cultures it is tradition for the names to be extra long.

Nether José nor María knew that one day, their child would grow up to be one of the most renowned artists in the entire world. Since José was an artist himself, he taught Pablo about drawing and painting from a remarkably young age. In fact, there is a story that says Pablo's first word was "*piz*."

Piz is what babies who speak Spanish would first call a *lapiz*, which means "pencil" in Spanish. From the moment Pablo Picasso could pick up a pencil, he loved to draw. He would draw on paper, he would draw on dirt, he would draw in sand—it was something he loved to do, and his father was very, very proud of him.

Both José and María encouraged Pablo to become an artist from a remarkably young age. He showed promise, and it was something that he clearly loved to do. José liked to take Pablo to bullfights, which is a popular Spanish tradition. In an arena, a professional bullfighter takes on a bull; this can be a fearfully dangerous situation, so only very skilled people did it. The crowd loved to see these types of shows, and bullfighting is still popular in Spain today. The man often has to escape the bull, but he tries to do it in the most daring and exciting ways possible, to keep the audience entertained and to keep them coming back for more.

Pablo loved to see the bullfights with his father, and when he got home he tried to sketch out some of the scenes that he saw. When he was eight years old, he made an attempt at one of his very first paintings, which was about bullfighting. His mother and father were incredibly impressed, and they showed it to all of their family and friends, who told their family and friends, who told *their* family and friends, and soon, everyone was talking about the eight-year old artist named Pablo Picasso.

Pablo Picasso grew up with two siblings. One of them was named Lola, and the other was named Conchita. However, Conchita did not live for unusually long. When she was seven years old, she passed away from diphtheria, a breathing infection. Obviously, the entire family was devastated, although Pablo was not really old enough to understand. Despite his young age, though, he became afraid of death. He had seen death take his younger sister, and this made him afraid of death. If his sister had suffered death, couldn't anyone else be next?

Despite the death of Conchita and his fear, a young Pablo Picasso still managed to get his name out into the world as a successful artist. When he was thirteen years old, he held his first art show, which is when all of his works were showcased to an audience. Many people believe that his father José was incredibly jealous of Pablo's work; while José had been working all of his life for success, becoming an art teacher, Pablo was thirteen and already having art shows. Even if he was jealous, however, he was still incredibly proud. He passed all of his brushes and other utensils onto Pablo and never made any works of art ever again.

Pablo Picasso applied to art school the next year, something that was usually reserved for college students only. However, because he was so talented, he was immediately accepted into their program. This was also the school that José taught at, so it would be nice for José and Pablo to be in the same school. Pablo and his family moved to the Spanish city of Barcelona, which is currently the second largest city in all of Spain. It sits on the banks of the Mediterranean Sea, which makes it a hugely popular destination for tourists to visit.

At the school, Pablo Picasso quickly became a favorite among the professors there. They loved seeing his talent and his enthusiasm for art each day; he was one of the best students in the entire school! At age fourteen, he was taking classes for only the most advanced artists, and he managed to keep a decent pace throughout the class. Pablo was talented way beyond his years.

When he was sixteen years old, he created a work of art called *Science and Charity*, which depicted his sister Lola sick in bed, his father José at her side. There will be more details about this painting later, but it is essential to understand that the painting was put on display in the Spanish capital of Madrid, where it won a truly special award! Pablo Picasso had not even reached eighteen years old, and yet he was still famous across the country of Spain. His artwork was placed beside the works of Spain's greatest artists; his talents compared with those who had worked with a brush for decades.

After *Science and Charity* was awarded in Madrid, José and María knew that their son could not remain in Barcelona. He was too talented. He had too bright of a future ahead of him—he needed to go somewhere else, to study among the greats, to show his true potential in the adult world. So where were they going to send him?

There was no better place than Madrid, a center for arts and science and culture in Spain. Pablo was sent to the Royal Academy of San Fernando, one of the most renowned schools in the entire country. However, as great of an artist as Pablo was, he was not the greatest student.

Pablo Picasso did not always attend each of his classes. Instead, he would skip them, which was against the rules. He also did not like the way that they thought art at the school. Many of his teachers made him copy notable examples from art history, which was a method that had been used for centuries. The teachers thought that, by copying examples from ancient history, the students would learn what good art really was. Pablo, however, disagreed with this idea.

Pablo wanted to learn by painting his own ideas and trying out different styles of art. This method, after all, was what led to such great success with many of his early paintings. He loved studying history and ancient artists and their work, but he also wanted to be independent from them. So, that was exactly what he would do.

However, Pablo Picasso did not last terribly long at the school. It was unfortunate timing; the next winter, he became sick with scarlet fever, which had infected many people at the time. He came down with a seriously sore throat and rashes across his body. He had to take time off from school while he was sick, and during this time he thought about what the future might hold for him.

When he became better, did he *really* want to return to art school? No, not really. He did not like it there. He did not like the teachers, and he did not like the way that they ran the class. The Royal Academy of San Fernando was just not the place for him. He was Pablo Picasso, and he was going to paint things the way he wanted to. His family expressed their disagreement; the Royal Academy was one of the best schools in all of Spain; how could he just throw away his education?

Pablo was not sorry for his decision. He was not going to let a school control his art. He was going to make his way out into the world and paint his own future.

Chapter 2: Picasso Explores the World

By the time that Picasso was nineteen years old, he was off on his own. His boring school life was behind him, and the world was in front of him, ready to be explored! He decided that he would actually like to return to Barcelona, since he had liked it so much more than Madrid. It was in Barcelona that Picasso became part of something called the Modernist movement—artists who painted things differently than they had ever been painted before.

One of the centers for the Modernist movement was a café called The Four Cats. Cafes were often breeding centers for art and culture, and at any time, one could find innovative artists inside. Pablo loved spending time inside The Four Cats, or, as it was officially called Els Quatre Gats in the language of Catalan, which is a variation of Spanish. Since The Four Cats was hugely supportive of growing artists in Spain, they let Pablo show off his work to many of the customers, who thought his art was fantastic. They had never seen anything like it!

And that was when the opportunity of a lifetime came. One of Pablo's paintings was about to make him world famous when officials in Paris, France decided that it was good off to be showcased at the World's Fair. The World's Fair is a collection of works from all across the world, and it is held in a different city and country every year. It was extremely convenient that this year, it was in Paris, France—just one country away from Spain. It would not be truly far for Pablo to travel.

But Pablo was not just excited about showing his art off to famous people from across the world—he was excited to explore! He had never been to Paris before, and he knew that, in the city, he would experience all new things. Paris was known around the world as one of the most popular places for artists to travel to.

He did not want to go to Paris alone, so he asked one of his old friends from art school to join him. His friend's name was Carles Casagemas, and he was just as excited as Pablo to live in Paris and explore the marvellous city.

Without wasting any time, Pablo and Carles were soon off to Paris, France. Paris is the capital of France, and it is most well known for the Eiffel Tower (along with its delicious French food!). Pablo and Carles shared an apartment together, but they did not have enough money to pay for an expensive, adequate apartment. Instead, they had an apartment where the walls were bare and blank. They did not have any money for furniture or any accessories, and they both thought that their apartment was abundantly plain.

Pablo decided that he would put his artistic talent to work. On the walls around the apartment, he painted tables, chairs, bookcases, and other furniture items, so that it looked like they had stuff around their apartment. During the night, Pablo and Carles slept peacefully in their homely apartment—by day, the two of them explored the wondrous city that is Paris.

All around Paris, there was plenty of art to see. Van Gogh had died ten years ago, and people around the world were beginning to become fascinated with his art—including Pablo Picasso. Paris was a place of inspiration for him. He visited museums and art shows and was inspired by all of the great works that he saw; he saw the Parisian countryside and lovely city and was taken aback by its beauty. He would often paint things that he saw in Paris, since he loved the city so much.

Pablo's time in Paris did not last terribly long. After Pablo had shown his art off to the world, the excitement in his life died down. He wished once again to see his homeland of Spain, and so did Carles, who had been enduring tough times apart from his girlfriend. When his girlfriend left Carles for good, Pablo and Carles decided that it was time to move back to Spain.

Despite the fact that Pablo Picasso had been having an incredible time in Paris, France, his family was quite skeptical of his progress. When he returned home to visit his parents, his hair was long, and he was dressed fancily, like many of the Parisians. His parents were afraid that his work was making him forget his Spanish heritage. Would he still become the celebrated painter they thought he would be? Sure, his artwork had just been displayed in Paris—but what would happen next?

Because he did not want to disappoint his mother and father, he moved from Barcelona back to Madrid. Each day, he kept up painting and drawing for practice. He worked for magazines, he worked for newspapers—until something terrible happened.

Carles, Pablo's best friend, had been having a very hard time. He was depressed and distraught and eventually committed suicide over a broken heart. Pablo was horrified over the event; it was totally unexpected. Pablo was especially sad that, in Carles's final days and months, he had not been very present as a friend.

Carles's death had a profound impact on Pablo Picasso's life. Pablo started to paint with many more blue colors. Why is this so important? What does the color blue mean in a painting? This is crucial to understand, especially if you want to understand hidden meanings in art. Blue is a color that is typically associated with sadness, so people knew that something was wrong in his life.

To deal with his sorrow, Pablo painted some pictures of Carles. They were all heavily tainted with the color blue, and Pablo even admitted that there was a clear link between the use of the color blue in his art and Carles. Many historians even call this time in Pablo Picasso's life the "Blue Period," since he used the color so much. It is no coincidence that the color "blue" also means "sad" or "feeling down."

Pablo was unsure of what to do next, now that Carles was gone. He spent a lot of time traveling back and forth between cities, mainly Paris and Barcelona. He could not afford consistent homes, so he often found himself living in either inadequate hotels—either that, or apartments that were old and unsafe.

Once again, Pablo genuinely wanted someone to live with—so he asked another one of his artist friends to live with him. His name was Max Jacobs, and he specialized in writing poetry. Both Pablo and Max were working to make a hard living as artists—Pablo often had to work overnight because there simply weren't enough hours in the day.

Pablo was running out of money. He did not have the money to find a steady home, and he most certainly did not have the money to purchase enough proper art supplies. While many painters used canvases to take down their work, Pablo did not have enough money. He had to use paper instead of canvases.

So, what types of things did Picasso like to paint? The poor and the disabled interested Picasso, so he would often paint them. He would paint homeless people that he found living on the streets of Paris and Barcelona. He would visit prisons and paint and draw images of the prisoners.

During this time in Picasso's life, he was terribly sad. His best friend had died, and interest in his art was lacking. People were not buying his art like he thought they would; sure, his art had been displayed in Paris. But something was wrong—if his art was so good, why were people not buying it? Pablo's parents were convinced that it had something to do with his time spent in Paris. They told him that he should not paint any more blue paintings; obviously, people did not want to buy them.

Chapter 3: Picasso Grows Into An Artist

No matter what people thought of him and his art, Pablo Picasso continued to do what he thought was right. Who cares if people didn't like his blue paintings? Who cares if his parents thought his career was going downhill? Eventually, things started to look a bit brighter for Picasso—in his life, and in his art.

He realized that he *really* liked Paris—way better than Barcelona. Paris was just such an amazing center of art and culture. It is impossible to deny Paris's importance in Picasso's life since it had such a profound impact and influence on his art. He decided that he wanted to stay in Paris—but not just temporarily. He wanted to live there permanently, he liked it so much. He knew that Paris was the city that would change his life, that would truly make him happy.

If you compare Picasso's paintings when he was traveling to his paintings when he was living in Paris, there is a noticeable difference. Not only do his later paintings contain more bright and lively colors, but they just seem happier. It is almost as if the viewer can see Picasso's smiling, focused face looking at his work as he determinedly makes each brushstroke.

If Pablo Picasso had just been living in a time that historians call the "Blue Period," he was now living in the "Rose Period," since the color of a rose is much happier color. It is also appropriate that the rose is a symbol of love, for Picasso's love life was also looking up. Although he had never had too much luck and experience with the ladies, he found great partnership in Fernande Olivier, who was a fellow artist. Picasso she thought she was absolutely gorgeous, and the two of them got along together.

Pablo and Fernande could think of no place better to live in Paris, in a large apartment house that was full of other artists. Even though the house was not in the best shape, and even though it was falling apart in some places, Pablo and Fernande were happy where they were.

All of the artists inside the apartment house were excited to be living with *the* Pablo Picasso. He was something of a rising star as his paints become more and more famous. He was coming along, slowly but surely. But his paintings were not the only thing that made him an intriguing person.

Pablo Picasso was very smart. He liked to have interesting, intellectual discussions that involved a lot of thought and wonder. By no means was he a boring person. Everyone loved talking with him and being around him. They genuinely felt like he was one of the important people of the time; little did they know, Pablo Picasso's art would go on to change the world.

There were two people in particular that recognized the importance of Pablo Picasso's work. The Steins, a pair of siblings from America, instantly became great friends with Picasso. The brother's name was Leo Stein, and the sister's name was Gertrude Stein. The Steins loved art just as much as Picasso did, and they always invited artists over for dinner. When they invited Picasso to their house, he was absolutely thrilled. He felt like a celebrity!

But it did not end there. At the Steins' house, Picasso met his idol. He met Henri Matisse, one of the most famous artists of the time period, and Picasso's favorite painter. It was the equivalent of, today, a child meeting their favorite movie star or television show character. Pablo Picasso was instantly enthralled; he had met his favorite painter of all time, who had inspired much of his work and convinced him to keep on painting, no matter what.

Henri Matisse, as well, instantly took a liking to the young and enthusiastic Pablo Picasso. Since the two of them were artists, they competed with each other for fame and money—just like two bands or two television shows might compete against each other today. However, despite this, Matisse and Picasso recognized the brilliance of each other's work and shared an uncommonly deep friendship.

At one of these dinner events, Pablo and Gertrude Stein agreed that he would attempt to create a painting of her. Surely this would be absolutely no trouble for the talented and skilled Picasso. However, the painting ended up being much more of a challenge than he had originally thought. He messed up on the face once and started over—and then he messed up again and started over—and then he messed up again—he did this eighty times. Picasso was flustered, and even Gertrude Stein was becoming slightly impatient.

Eventually, Picasso finished Gertrude's portrait, but he was decidedly displeased with his work. Did this really look like her? Would people like his painting? Would people think that he was a poor painter and never want to buy his art again? Many of Picasso's followers thought that the painting bore remarkably little resemblance to Gertrude, but Gertrude was not so critical. She told him that she loved it—she had such an interest in the young Picasso that she probably would have liked anything he had drawn.

This led Picasso to a very important realization. He had tried eighty times to paint Gertrude Stein's face—why did he keep on failing? How could he become better? Was it skill that needed work, or was it his perspective? A *perspective* is the way in which someone looks at something. Picasso realized that he was having so much trouble with Gertrude's portrait because he was trying to get every single little detail to be painted as accurately as possible. But what if things did not *need* to be that way? What if he could paint what he saw in his *mind*, and not what he saw with his *eyes*?

Picasso changed the way he painted, and this led to a huge success in his art career. He was no longer focused on the details, and this allowed him to expand his creativity. He enjoyed painting much more, and people enjoyed his work much more too. It was a win-win situation! The money was pouring in, which made him and Fernande supremely happy. They were able to afford more things, live in a better, adequate house, and even go on scenic vacations. However, their relationship did not last much longer. Picasso was enticed by Fernande's beauty, but he no longer liked her as a person. It was not long before he had a new girlfriend.

As Picasso's personal life was changing, so was his artistic career. He liked to explore different artistic methods and techniques with many of the artists that he hung around with. One of his greatest friends was a man by the name of Georges Braque. Together, Picasso and Braque invented a technique of art that is used in schools across the country and across the world. Perhaps you have even done this yourself! It is called a "collage." The word "collage" is a French word that means "to stick."

Picasso and Braque would occasionally paste items onto their paintings, such as texts from newspapers and magazines. Instead of painting certain things, they thought that using real-world items would send a greater message and truly make their work come alive. Now, collages are made in classrooms and in workplaces across the world—all thanks to Pablo Picasso and Georges Braque!

Chapter 4: Picasso Steps Onto the World Stage

Picasso lived during a hugely important time in the world's history—he saw World War I erupt across the globe as countries pointed fingers at each other, took sides, made allies, and declared war. A man from Serbia assassinated Archduke Franz Ferdinand from Austria, and soon enough, Serbia and Austria were at each other's throats. The large country of Russia wanted to protect Serbia's actions, while Germany immediately flew to Austria's side. Germany was incensed by Russia; how could they possibly take Serbia's side? So Germany issued an official declaration of war on Russia.

So how was Picasso involved in all of this? Well, after France issued a statement declaring its support for Serbia and Russia, Germany declared war on France too. It was not long before the United States of America, along with several other countries around the world, were dragged into the conflict. The entire world was at war with itself for the first time.

This all happened in the year 1914, when Picasso and Braque were still living in France. While the war did not have an enormous and immediate effect on Picasso, it did have a vital part to play in Braque's life. The French government issued a *draft*, which is when they force citizens to join the military. The United States has not issued a draft since the 1970s during the Vietnam War, and the whole idea of a draft has become generally unpopular. But World War I and World War II saw many drafts and France was one country that supported them.

Braque was forced into the military, but Picasso was not. Why not? Picasso was technically not a French citizen, so the French government could not force him to serve in their army. While Braque and many of Picasso's friends went off to fight Germany and Austria, Picasso remained in France.

The war raised some truly interesting questions in France. For starters, the man that owned a gallery with Picasso's work in it was a German man. France was at war with Germany, so they immediately saw the gallery owner as an enemy and a potential spy. The French government wanted to take no chances, so they deported him and took all of the art inside the gallery—this included many of Picasso's famous pieces of art.

As Picasso saw the world around him falling apart, so too did his love life fall apart. His new girlfriend, Eva Gouel, came down with a terrible sickness called tuberculosis. While today there may be many medicines and treatments that a person can take for tuberculosis, at the start of the twentieth century, medicine was not as advanced. Unfortunately, Eva passed away, leaving Picasso absolutely devastated.

His friends were all away at war, and he was at home alone. His girlfriend had just died. Things were not going well in Picasso's life, and this once again reflected in his paintings. Picasso was sad, but he hoped that things would eventually get better.

He did not spent the entirety of World War I stuck in Paris, France, however. He actually traveled to Rome, a very famous city in Italy! While in Paris, he met a poet by the name of Jean Cocteau, who had risen to fame because his work was so likable and relatable. Like most people, Jean Cocteau adored Pablo Picasso. Cocteau knew that Picasso was extremely intelligent, very creative, and very friendly as well—despite the war raging to the east, and the effect it had on Picasso.

Jean Cocteau wanted to work on something with Picasso, but painting was not actually his expertise. Cocteau had been working with a ballet lately, and he thought it would be fantastic if Picasso could help out! When Picasso asked what the play was called and what it was about, Cocteau told him that it was called "Parade," and that it was about an extravagant circus!

Picasso immediately saw that he could be exceptionally creative with this project, and that was something that he liked. He had some doubts though, especially because he had never even seen a ballet before in his lifetime. Still, he took the challenge on. It would give him a chance to do something other than painting, and he would be able to travel to Rome!

Picasso's part in the project was to design the costumes and the set pieces for the ballet. He thought he did an excellent job, and he could not wait for people to see his work!

When opening night came, both Picasso and Cocteau were incredibly nervous. What would people think? Would they like the costumes? The play? After the first performance of the ballet, the audience was not too sure they liked it. The costumes were extravagant—a little *too* extravagant for the public's liking. It was like nothing they had ever seen before, and they did not like this. The play was overwhelming, so the general reaction was quite negative.

Obviously, Picasso and Cocteau were a little disappointed by this news, especially after how much effort they had put into creating the costumes and the set pieces. He decided that maybe ballets were not his area of expertise, so he decided to move away from them—however, there was something (or some*one*) about the ballet he could not get out of his mind.

It was a woman, and her name was Olga Khokhlova. She had been a dancer in the ballet, and throughout the entire experience, Picasso had absolutely fascinated with her beauty. He thought that she had been the most gorgeous ballet dancer in the entire production, and he revealed his interest in her. About one year after they had met each other, Pablo Picasso and Olga Khokhlova were married.

Olga was incredibly rich. She had friends in the high tiers of society. She always attended ballets and balls and wore all the newest fashions. People talked about her beauty and her riches. This was an incredibly different experience for Picasso. Just a few years ago, he was living in an apartment building that was falling apart, and now he was attending dances in fancy suits.

Pablo felt rather uncomfortable among the rich elite of Parisian society. All of his life, he had been a man of the poor and the working class. Many of his paintings depicted the lives of the homeless and those who struggled to survive—and here he was with more money than he knew what to do with, more food than he could eat, and more clothes than he could wear. Was this right for him to do?

A few years after Picasso and Olga got married, World War I ended with Germany and Austria standing disgraced and defeated, many other countries emerging as victors. Picasso was happy when all of his old friends returned home, but Olga did not like it when Picasso hung out with his friends. Many of them were not rich, and they were not proper; so why should her husband be with them? Picasso did not like it when she told him that, and, unfortunately, he went with the flow and did not see his friends as often.

It was not long before Olga became pregnant, and a new, smiling face joined their household. They named their new son Paulo when he was born in 1921. Pablo was the proudest father on the face of the earth, and he let everyone know. Several times he created paintings of Olga and Paulo together, happy.

Many people noticed a difference in his paintings of Olga and Paulo. We will talk more about this later, but most of Pablo Picasso's work tended to be hugely blocky, plain, and occasionally difficult to understand. His depictions of Olga and Paulo, however, were painted in much detail and truly lifelike.

For a while, things seemed to be going well for Pablo Picasso, despite the fact that he and Olga were not the best match. He could never get accustomed to her fancy way of living, and she was often rude to him. They eventually stopped sleeping together, and then she started criticizing his art and his studio. Picasso, like many famous artists, was not the most organized person, and his art studio was almost never neat. Picasso liked things like that, but Olga could not say the same. She kept on telling him to clean up his mess and, of course, he absolutely refused.

Enough was enough. Picasso had had enough of Olga, and he told her so when he purchased another house and left her. The house was still in Paris, although on the northern side, and Picasso hoped that it would be a decent enough escape for Olga. As had often happened with Picasso, it was not long before he had his sights set on someone else.

Marie-Therese Walter and Pablo Picasso had met in the Paris subway, and Picasso was instantly entranced with her. She was absolutely beautiful! As he had done with Olga and Paulo, Picasso enjoyed painting pictures of Marie-Therese. He simply could not get enough of her and, eventually, the two of them shared a daughter together. They named the girl Maya, and Picasso enjoyed painting pictures of her too.

But soon enough, another lady entered Picasso's life. Her name was Dora Maar, and she was a photographer. Picasso instantly fell in love with Dora, and soon he was faced with a predicament. He loved Marie-Therese, he loved Dora, and Olga was still trying to talk to him. What was he supposed to do? He now had two children with two different women. His problems were growing by the day, and he was not sure if there was any clear way out.

He decided that he wanted to be with Dora, but, after a while, he found that even his love for her was slowly dying. What was he supposed to do now? He met another woman, by the name of Françoise Gilot, who he *truly* fell in love with—hopefully. Picasso decided he liked her better than any of the other women, but how long that love would last no one could actually tell.

But, for the most part, it was very difficult for Picasso to focus on his love life. After all, he was alive at a time when the world was changing each and every day. Spain was erupting into a bloody civil battle, and the world was plunging into the climactic World War II.

Chapter 5: Picasso's World at War

After World War I, in the decade of the 1920s, Picasso spent most of his time in Paris. He experimented with different writing styles and dealt with his many romantic and family issues. This took up a lot of time and, about fifteen years later, in the year 1936, something terrible happened in Pablo Picasso's home country of Spain.

There was a military general, Francisco Franco, who overthrew the government, using the army to take the entire country hostage. Franco believed in a *fascist* government. *Fascism* is a type of government in which a single person—a *dictator*—controls everything in a country, and the people are not allowed to disagree with him. It is the opposite of freedom and liberty. The people of Spain were divided. Some people liked this new form of government, and others wanted to fight back against Franco and the Spanish army. Thus erupted the Spanish Civil War.

Under this form of government, and because battles were taking place throughout Spain each day, it was impossible for Picasso to go back home. It absolutely devastated him, and every single day he wished for the war to end and his people to be free.

The Spanish Civil War led to one of Picasso's most famous paintings. It was called *Guernica*, and perhaps you have even seen it before! There is a interesting story behind the painting.

In 1937, a year after the war had begun, Germany entered the war. Germany was under the rule of the fascist dictator Adolf Hitler, one of the villainous and infamous people in all of world history. Hitler had taken charge of Germany after World War I and saved the country of a horrible economic tragedy; the people of Germany loved Hitler for saving them; even though he made some bad decisions and prosecuted Jewish citizens, he was allowed to rise to the position of Fuhrer—the German word for "leader." In fact, Hitler is now considered to evil that the word "Fuhrer" is now defined as a tyrannous ruler.

German airplanes flew over the town of Guernica in northern Spain. No one had expected the attack, because there was no reason for Germany to interfere in Spain's civil war. The German planes soared over Guernica's streets and dropped bombs rapidly. Explosions erupted into the air, children and women and men screamed, animals ran everywhere, and entire buildings and roads were shattered to pieces.

The death count ran over one thousand six hundred people. Over nine hundred Spanish citizens suffered tough injuries. The Spanish rebellion was absolutely devastated; Franco and his German allies had won a great victory.

Picasso knew where Guernica was; it was even close to where he grew up as a child. He did not know how to understand this attack, how so many people could die so quickly, in such a desperate act of hatred. He did not want to flock to Spain to fight; how could he support his people from the safe confines of Paris, France?

He picked up the brush and readied himself to paint, and he began work on one of the most famous paintings of all time. It stood at an astounding twelve feet tall, more than three times the height of an average man; it also ran twenty-six feet long. He worked day and night, sometimes for hours at a time, relentlessly on *Guernica.*

Three weeks later, he put down the brush. Dora had supported him wholeheartedly throughout the project, and with a camera she took many photos of both Picasso painting it, and the painting itself.

Guernica is a painting that depicts suffering and pain. It is supposed to show the tragedy of the Guernica bombing, and it clearly conveys all of the emotions and destruction. When the painting was revealed to the public, it was very clear what it supposed to portray. People were very moved by all of the different events in the painting, the screaming people, the running animals, and the severed body parts. Everything in the painting seemed distorted and improper, which demonstrated how panicked everything was during the bombing.

While the war raged through 1937 and 1938, the year 1939 brought a whole new conflict. For months, Hitler had slowly been conquering more territories in Europe. Germany was ruled by a government referred to as the *Third Reich*, and Hitler's Third Reich was becoming supreme. He outlined and publicly professed his plans to conquer the nation of Poland, planning to "cleanse" the country of its Jewish citizens.

However, other countries were tired of Hitler's antics and his rising power. Once Hitler's armies moved toward Poland, the next world war finally erupted. The United States of America, England, France, and many other countries stood against the ruthless German Third Reich.

The French were terrified of a German bombing attack. What if the Germans bombed France like they had bombed Spain? What would happen if people died by the thousands, like they already had in other countries under attack from the Third Reich? Men like Picasso wondered what would happen if a museum was bombed—would all his art be simply destroyed in a matter of minutes? Museums across France shut down and locked up their art, determined to stand strong against Germany.

Picasso and his family gathered together and moved farther away into southern Spain; it was dangerous to be too close to Germany, in the case of an attack. However, as Picasso's family soon discovered, France could not hold out against the strong German forces. The Germans defeated the French in battle and, within days, German tanks were rolling down the streets of Paris, and the flags of the Third Reich were flying from buildings everywhere.

This news was absolutely devastating to Pablo Picasso. Paris! The city he had loved and live for was now under control by the enemy. What was he going to do? Should he stay in Spain, under the fascist control of Francisco Franco? Or should he return to Paris, under the iron fist of Adolf Hitler?

Proudly, with his chin held high in the air, and with his belongings with him, Pablo Picasso marched into the German-occupied city of Paris, France. Hitler's soldiers, called the Nazis (naht-zees), patrolled the streets and buildings everywhere. With him, Picasso took all of his painting materials. He might not fight World War II with a gun, but he would most certainly fight with his paintbrush and with his mind.

Under the Nazi regime in Paris, life was very difficult. The Nazis were at war with the Parisians, and the Parisians were technically their prisoners. The citizens were treated kindly. Laws were stricter. Food was scarce. People lived in fear of Hitler and his soldiers, even more so now that his soldiers were marching outside their homes.

The Nazis knew that Picasso was living in Paris, and they also knew that he was the one that painted *Guernica*. They knew that he did not like them and that he was interested in painting messages against them. Picasso would often hear loud banging on his door, only to find Nazi soldiers present to interrogate them. They accused him of being Jewish, and it was law that Jewish citizens were not equal to others. Already, the Third Reich had unjustly killed millions of Jewish people.

Picasso was not Jewish, however, and the Nazis could not arrest him. However, they had more than enough reason to imprison based on his opposition to their regime. If Picasso stood defiantly against the Third Reich, using his paintbrush as his sword, couldn't they just arrest him and put an end to his art? Well, some historians believe that officials in the Third Reich wanted to protect Picasso because they knew he was so famous. If they arrested, imprisoned, or even killed Picasso, it might make the German people angry, and that could be a threat to Hitler's power. So, Picasso was allowed to live safely under the German occupation of Paris—but the Nazis kept a particularly close eye on him and his work.

Much of Picasso's work showed the struggling poor. He wanted to give hope to the lower classes, showing them that people did recognize their troubles and that, one day, they might rise up against oppressors like Hitler. While Picasso fought the war from the safety of his house, battles were brewing in the streets of Paris.

French rebels launched an attack against the German soldiers in Paris, and they were joined by French and American soldiers marching into the city. Planes soared over Paris, American tanks plowed through the streets, and gunfire exploded around every corner. The Germans were no match for the combined forces of both France and the United States, and Germany soon surrendered Paris.

Picasso was thrilled when he realized that Paris was saved at last! He opened his doors and felt free, and the American and French soldiers were amazed to meet him. This was *the* Pablo Picasso, whose art had held out hope for many during the course of the war. He let soldiers take shelter and sleep in his house, and he was more than happy to show off his art to the men who had freed Paris.

World War II began in 1939, and it ended six years later in 1945. Throughout the war, people around the war had celebrated his art as standing against fascism and oppression, fighting both Franco's forces and Hitler's slowly-crumbling Third Reich.

Chapter 6: The End of Picasso's Life

Throughout World War II, and eight years after, Picasso spent his romantic life with Françoise. But, like all of his other relationships, it was not long before it fell apart. This time, though, it was Françoise who left him, and not the other way around. Picasso was shocked! Why would someone ever leave him?

But also like all of the other cases, Picasso quickly found another woman to fall in love with. Her name was Jacqueline, and they remained in France after they got married. Some people might think this is strange today, but Picasso married her when he was eighty years old! He loved her, and he thought they would make a great husband and wife. He did not care about his age, he just wanted to get married.

After World War II, Picasso had become absolutely famous. Buildings, cafes, museums, and schools across the world showed his art. His name was everywhere! Historians and scholars were always talking about him, his art, and the way it had impacted the Spanish Civil War and World War II.

Even at the old age of eighty, he painted day and night. He had painted well over one thousand paintings—he painted over one hundred of his wife Jacqueline alone—and many people revered him for this. As he got older, he painted more; mainly because his wisdom and experience had made him want to send out more messages. He wanted to paint and talk with people more, despite getting older.

He even managed to hit his ninetieth birthday. However, he had been suffering many health problems recently, and doctors were not sure how much longer he would last. On April 8th of 1973, Picasso lay sick and dying and bed, with a doctor by his side doing all he could to help. Right before Picasso died, he turned to the doctor and with his dying breaths, he spoke the words:

"Drink to me, drink to me health; you know I can't drink anymore."

The doctor reported these words to the public along with the news of his death, and the entire world began mourning. His wife Jacqueline and his children were devastated, along with all of his former girlfriends and wives. Around the world, tributes to Picasso and his art went up. Sales of his art increased exponentially, although of only a choice few; Picasso created, throughout his entire lifetime, fifty thousand work of art, each of them unique and well thought out.

Around the world, entire museums have been dedicated to preserving and showing off only Picasso's work, such as the Picasso Museum in Barcelona and the Picasso Museum in France.

Now that we have studied the life of the artist, we must understand his art. What *about* his art made it so influential? Where does his art rest within artistic culture and movements?

Chapter 7: The Eternal Art of Pablo Picasso

The world of art had been changing long before Picasso was born, and it continued to change throughout his lifetime. For a while, artists had been challenging existing "rules" of art, by experimenting and creating new ways of painting. Vincent van Gogh, for example, headed many efforts to paint differently as part of a *post-modernist movement.* We call the artists that tried to change the face of the artistic world *modernists.*

Pablo Picasso was very much a *modernist* artist. He took art into the new age through creative thinking and intriguing viewpoints. For example, some historians say that his painting "Les Demoiselles D'Avignon" is one of his top five famous painting of all time. The picture shows five women, one of them with an African tribal mask, is strange poses.

The details of the painting are by no means realistic. Unfortunately, this is what many people still wanted; they wanted to be able to live inside the painting through vivid details. For centuries, men before Picasso had been creating paintings that were lifelike (Leonardo da Vinci is still famous for his realistic and detailed paintings, such as the Mona Lisa).

Picasso was a little disappointed by the reaction to his painting. His style is very unique, and one must truly see it, and research to understand what it is like. Some of the time, his paintings are majorly blocky with clear defined lines that do not actually appear as such in real life.

Why did Picasso do this? If many people wanted him to paint realistic drawings, why did he not do that? It was not because he could not paint lifelike drawings. He most certainly could, and he *did*, of his many girlfriends.

Picasso thought differently than other people. He was one of the greatest artistic minds of the twentieth century, and he wanted to paint the women in a way different than people might automatically expect. His art was two-dimensional, which means it looked flat and as if it had no real depth; but was the point to create a lifelike drawing? What is the message of Les Demoiselles d'Avignon?

Many art scholars have noted the odd way in which many of the women in the painting are twisting their bodies, exposing some parts while hiding others. What is the purpose of this? Some believe that Picasso is trying to show different parts of the female body in different places, in a truly creative way. Whatever he was trying to accomplish, he was certainly successful in attracting attention. While many scholars used to denounce the painting as an insult to the world of art, others have called it one of the greatest paintings of the twentieth century.

As Picasso continued to experiment with the paintbrush, especially his friend Braque, whose talent almost matched his, he began to realize that he was on the brink of inventing a new style of art altogether. Unlike most other paintings of the time, but like Les Demoiselles d'Avignon, Picasso liked to segment the things in his work into shapes like squares and circles. It was very different, and nobody had painted like this before!

This style quickly became known as *cubism*, and it was Picasso's signature trademark. The reaction to cubism at first was divided. It was so different that some people had trouble understanding his paintings and forming proper opinions.

When Picasso began painting pictures of his girlfriends and his wives, it was hugely important that they were not painted in cubist form. He instead painted them very lifelike and detailed, exactly as he saw them. His other work, however, was intended to serve as how he thought about things and how he looked out at the world. The loves of his life, however, were too beautiful not to be depicted exactly as they were. When you think about it, it is rather sweet!

Another one of Picasso's famous paintings is called "The Two Saltimbanques." Instantly, the moment you see the painting, you can tell that the two figures in it are truly said. This was painted during the time period of Picasso's life called the Blue Period, when he was very depressed. There is a heavy amount of blue in the painting, and it seems to embody all the sad and negative emotions that Picasso must have been enduring as he struggled through his early years.

"Saltimbanques" is the French word for "acrobats," which is extremely intriguing. The painting has nothing to do with acrobats, and from the very look of it, you would never know that the two people sadly sitting in the painting are acrobats. It is possible that Picasso was showing them not doing their job because they were sad, or possibly because they could never live up to expectations. If there is a painting that represents Picasso's Blue Period, it is this one.

When Pablo Picasso's good friend Carlos Casegemas committed suicide one year, during Picasso's Blue Period, Picasso was obviously very upset and disturbed. In order to rid himself of his sadness and frustration, he turned to the paintbrush and painted "The Old Guitarist." Most of the painting was created with varying shades of blue, depicting an elderly man hunched over his guitar. The picture is very sad because it seems as if the man can barely play, and is old and weak. This painting is also a strong representation of the Blue Period. "The Old Guitarist" is one of Picasso's paintings that did not involve the style of cubism.

One of Picasso's later paintings, called "Weeping Woman," depicts a woman's face in intense pain. It was not created during the Blue Period, but rather during the Spanish Civil War and two years before the outbreak of World War II. Many people think it is face of Dora Maar, one of Picasso's girlfriends. Allegedly, he would always call her the "weeping woman." Whether this is true or not remains to be seen. This was painted around the time of the Guernica bombing, so it is possible that it is just Picasso focusing all of his anger, frustration, and sadness into one painting. Nevertheless, even though the painting is unrealistic and strictly cubist, it is disturbing and touching. It truly has to be seen to be understood.

One of Picasso's final works is also one of his most famous. It is called *Self Portrait Facing Death*, and it is a self-portrait of Picasso. It can sometimes be hard to tell exactly who Picasso is trying to paint, especially because of his cubist style. It is terribly important to know that when Picasso painted this, he was near his death, around ninety years old. He knew that death was coming sooner or later, and he obviously needed to grapple with many issues that surrounds nearing death. How should be approach death? Should he be afraid? Should he succumb to fear, or should he stand brave against the end of his life?

Even though the self-portrait is painted in a cubist style, and even though it is not supposed to look realistic, a viewer can still see what Picasso thought of his approach to death. Scholars have been varying opinions on the painting. Picasso's eyes in the painting are unusually wide and open as if he is afraid, but other scholars think that he is looking death in the face with courage and valor. *Self-Portrait Facing Death*, however, was not the final self-portrait Picasso created.

There were others, many of them much more disturbing and senseless. Some of them were not cubist at all, but rather bland, consisting of black and white. This is what Picasso thought of himself as he faced death. It was not colorful and happy, like some of his other paintings. It was not blue and solemn, like the works of the Blue Period. The final self-portraits were disturbing and interestingly human. While they make not make sense at first, once the audience truly takes the time to think about each painting not literally, but figuratively, then they can mean so much more.

Picasso is blessed with a rare honor: his place in history is well-known and significant. Many artists have had a tremendously strong effect on culture and artistic movements, but Picasso's hand was very powerful in the politics of the Spanish Civil War and World War II. While many artists talk about life, Picasso used his art to inspire rebels and to give hope to those who thought that hope was lost.

The period of the Spanish Civil War and World War II is one of the most desperate and devastating times in world history, a time when a line was drawn in the sand between good and evil, when Picasso looked out his window and saw Nazi soldiers marching down the streets, when he heard of his own cities under attack, when he knew that his art was changing lives. Around the world, people looked at his art, and they saw a human struggle. They saw the devastation of *Guernica* and realized that the bombing was severe and terrible. It was a way of drawing attention to the rebels' cause and the destruction caused by the German army.

Like many artists around the world and throughout history, Picasso used connections with other artists to develop his skills. Braque, Casagemas, and others helped Picasso create the style of cubism. Cubism still remains as one of the most creative and lasting styles of the modernist art era.

Picasso absolutely revolutionized the world of art in the 1900s. While many people thought that artists needed to depict life as we saw it with our eyes, he knew that he could paint things as he saw them in his head. His thoughts and feelings were just as influential, perhaps more important than what he saw with his eyes. He knew that he would be able to convey more emotion, and deeper messages if his own feelings were able to bleed through the painting—and that is where cubism helped him.

Of all the artists of the twentieth century, Picasso stands out as being one of the most, if not *the* most, influential. His work against the Spanish fascists and the Nazi regime was critical is creating a culture that served to keep the hopes of rebels strong. Picasso's world was one of danger and death. He lived through bombings. He lived in a city under occupation by the world's most terrifying and feared army. And yet he lived to tell the story and even painted a few hours before his death at ninety-one years old.

There are many lessons to take away from Picasso, and not all of them have to do with artistic style. There is always hope, Picasso told us, whether you are fighting a war with a sword or a paintbrush. He did his part to help make the world a better place. His art is still observed and studied across the world. As long as there are wars, and as long as there is art in human society, Picasso will have a tremendously important place in our history.

Resources

Kelley, True. *Who Was Pablo Picasso?* New York: Grosset & Dunlap, 2009. Print.

https://geniusmothers.com/genius-mothers-of/famous-artists-writers-musicians/Maria-Picasso-Lopez/

http://web.org.uk/picasso/occupation.html

http://www.nytimes.com/learning/general/onthisday/big/0825.html

http://www.picasosgallery.com/pablo-picassos-most-famous-works.php

http://faculty.mdc.edu/nrodrigu/demoiselles/lesdemoiselles.htm

http://www.inminds.com/weeping-woman-picasso-1937.html

Printed in Great Britain
by Amazon